Psalms for Singing

Psalms for Singing

Twenty-six Psalms with Musical Settings
for Congregation and Choir

Translation of Psalms
by
Gary Chamberlain

The Upper Room
Nashville, Tennessee

Psalms for Singing

Book design: Linda Bryant

Library of Congress Catalog Card Number: 84-50778

First printing: April, 1984 (10)

ISBN: 0-8358-0495-X

Printed in the United States of America

Contents

Preface

Christians have claimed through the centuries that the psalms are the foundation of our praise and our hymnody, but in recent years all too little use of them has been made in our worship. There has been widespread dissatisfaction with the kind of chanting, metrical psalms, and responsive readings that have been our chief ways of using the psalms. Many have been convinced that there must surely be a way of praying and singing the psalms that is expressive of the "heart language" and musical styles of contemporary churchgoers.

The 1980 General Conference of The United Methodist Church directed the Board of Discipleship to do preparatory work toward a new official hymn and worship book and to make a report on this work to the 1984 General Conference. This work was directed to include "development, trial publication, and field testing, with suitable research, of a version of the Psalter suitable for United Methodist use."

As the Section on Worship of the Board of Discipleship conducted research on the psalter, it was evident that there is widespread dissatisfaction among United Methodists both with the psalter in the back of the present hymnal and with the limited opportunities to sing the psalms. A new translation of the psalms was commissioned and is being published in text form for reading. In this same new translation, certain psalms, long associated with Sunday worship, were selected to be set to music that would be singable by the average United Methodist congregation. Composers were contacted, and some of the more promising musical settings of these psalms are included here. To help the local church teach congregations the psalms, a tape will be made available which includes many of the musical settings published in *Psalms for Singing* with a commentary on introducing the music.

This resource has lectionary references at the end of each psalm, a Numerical Psalms Index with lectionary references, and a separate Seasonal Lectionary Index. All lectionary references are based upon *Seasons of the Gospel* (Abingdon Press, 1979), since the new Trial Common Lectionary has not yet been officially adopted. There are references made to the psalms in the book which appear in other musical settings in the supplemental music resources—*Supplement to the Book of Hymns, Songs of Zion, Celebremos,* and *Hymns from the Four Winds.*

7

Members of the Psalms Task Force responsible for the selection of psalms and music in *Psalms for Singing* are Gary Chamberlain, Roger Deschner, Elise Eslinger, Richard Eslinger, John Holbert, and Sylvia Scott of the United Church of Canada. Great appreciation is expressed to Jane Marshall who acted as a consultant for the project and to Lynn Cheshier, consultant in the Section on Worship, and Beverly Clement, graduate intern for the Section on Worship, who worked as assistant musical editors.

It should be stressed that this book is only a beginning. It is hoped that local churches using this book will send their reactions to the Section on Worship, P.O. Box 840, Nashville, Tennessee 37202. In the next hymnal, or when we next publish musical settings of psalms, we hope to have learned from this trial publication and testing.

JUDY L. LOEHR, PROJECT DIRECTOR
Director of Church Music and
   Worship Resources
Section on Worship
Board of Discipleship

HOYT L. HICKMAN
Assistant General Secretary
Section on Worship
Board of Discipleship

March, 1984

Translator's Introduction

The selected psalm texts presented here were translated with several aims in mind. The most important are fidelity to the Hebrew original, clarity, rhythm for ease in reading and singing, and the use of inclusive language suitable for the liturgy of the church.

"Fidelity to the Hebrew" means specifically the attempt not only to render the meaning of the original words (a problem complicated enough, as students of Hebrew and text criticism will certainly know), but to do so in forms that approach those of Old Testament poetry. Obviously, "parallelism" is the most widely discussed aspect here. Hebrew poetry consists of (most often) pairs of lines whose thought or syntax stand in relation to one another. But in addition one must recognize a tendency toward terse expression of a rhythmic kind, and in that respect this translation seeks to be closer to the texture of the Hebrew.

Being terse and compact makes it more difficult to be clear. But clarity *on first reading* (rather than after some time for reflective pondering) is crucial for public worship. So the translation is not "word-for-word"; rather, line by line, I have tried to say in natural English what I find in the text.

If the attempt at fidelity made clarity more difficult, it simplified the problems of rhythm. Compact lines have fewer accents, and fewer unaccented syllables between accents. As the pointing of the text indicates, all lines have three or four accents, with no more than two unaccented syllables between them. Not only does this give choral or responsive reading more momentum, it has made possible the development of the new system for singing that is presented here along with this text. I am convinced that in this music we come far closer to the rhythms of Hebrew psalmody than has ever been done before in any Western language.

The final complication has been the necessity for responsible language that expresses the inclusive nature both of God and of the church. We have decided to retain the traditional "Lord" for the divine name, and have been faithful to the text where it uses metaphors of kingship to speak of God. But we have eliminated all gendered pronouns in speaking either of God or the congregation (any "he" or "his" in the text refers to the king of Israel/Judah). And in Psalm 2, I have expressed the feminine metaphor of God giving birth to the new monarch.

I wish to add only that my daily relationship with the Hebrew psalter over the seven years of this translation's development has been a blessing for which I am profoundly thankful. The gift of praying the psalter is God's gift of true prayer—the prayer that is answered in Jesus Christ.

GARY CHAMBERLAIN

10

Music Editor's Introduction

The uniqueness of this sampling of *Psalms for Singing* is found in the ease and convenience in which they may be learned and sung. The simple tunes—each reflecting the moods of praise, zeal, thanks trust, hope, peace, awe, petition, fear, anger, sadness—and the pointed texts immediately below the tunes afford the simplest possible way of executing the psalms. Repetition is the key element to the vitality of psalm-singing and a value which cannot be highlighted enough.

Based upon the steady pulse of regularly recurring beats, the psalm begins with the antiphon, moves without change of pace into the psalm verses, and back to the antiphon as indicated or desired. (The antiphon is included as an element of drama, to heighten the overall mood of the psalm, or to bring relief after many verse repetitions.) The beat remains the same. Syllables between beats (indicated by points, or dots, over the text) frequently feel best when sung as triplets.

While it is assumed that most congregations will sing in unison from the pages which make up the first section of this volume, and which may be photocopied without permission for greater accessibility by entire congregations, the full music section which makes up the second part of the volume may be used by choirs which desire to sing some, or all, of the verses and antiphons in harmony. The overall design of this volume and its contents is one intended to provide flexibility and clarity, while at the same time encouraging inventiveness.

The singing of these psalms should be an event of great joy for the congregation. That same joy should characterize their rehearsal as well. It is the desire of all whose efforts have gone into the preparation of this sampling that your use of these psalms will provide your worship event with a new and vital resource.

Your comments are invited as preparations begin in anticipation of a companion volume to *Psalms for Singing*.

JOHN ERICKSON

Numerical Psalms Index

Psalm 1	Fourth Sunday after the Epiphany A, B Sixth Sunday after the Epiphany C
Psalm 2	Last Sunday of the Epiphany/Transfiguration A
Psalm 8	First Sunday after Pentecost/Trinity Sunday C
Psalm 19	Third Sunday in Lent B
Psalm 23	Fourth Sunday in Lent A Fourth Sunday of Easter A, B Sunday between July 17 & 23, Inclusive, B Sunday between October 9 & 15, Inclusive, A
Psalm 24	Fourth Sunday in Advent A All Saints' Day A, B
Psalm 29	First Sunday after the Epiphany/Baptism of The Lord A, B, C
Psalm 46	Last Sunday after Pentecost/Christ the King C
Psalm 47	Seventh Sunday of Easter A, B, C
Psalm 51	Ash Wednesday A, B, C Fifth Sunday in Lent B Sunday between September 11 & 17, Inclusive, C
Psalm 63	Sunday between June 19 & 25, Inclusive, C (if after Trinity Sunday) Sunday between November 6 & 12, Inclusive, A Daily Morning Prayer
Psalm 67	Second Sunday after the Epiphany B Sixth Sunday of Easter C Sunday between August 14 & 20, Inclusive, A
Psalm 72	Second Sunday in Advent A The Epiphany A, B, C
Psalm 91	First Sunday in Lent C

Psalm 95	Third Sunday in Lent A
	Sunday between October 2 & 8, Inclusive, C
	Last Sunday after Pentecost/Christ the King A
Psalm 98	Christmas Eve/Day B
	Easter Vigil A, B, C
	Sixth Sunday of Easter B
	Sunday between November 13 & 19, Inclusive, C
Psalm 100	Fourth Sunday of Easter C
	Sunday between June 12 & 18, Inclusive, A
	(if after Trinity Sunday)
Psalm 103	Seventh Sunday after the Epiphany A
	Eighth Sunday after the Epiphany B
	Third Sunday in Lent C
	Sunday between September 11 & 17, Inclusive, A
Psalm 121	Sunday between October 16 & 22, Inclusive, C
Psalm 126	Second Sunday in Advent C
	Sunday between October 23 & 29, Inclusive, B
Psalm 130	First Sunday in Lent A
Psalm 137	Fourth Sunday in Lent B
Psalm 139	Third Sunday of Easter B
Psalm 141	Daily Evening Prayer
Psalm 148	Second Sunday of Easter B
Psalm 150	First Sunday after Pentecost/Trinity Sunday A

Seasonal Lectionary Index

ADVENT

Second Sunday in Advent A	Psalm 72
Second Sunday in Advent C	Psalm 126
Fourth Sunday in Advent A	Psalm 24

CHRISTMAS

Christmas Eve/Day B	Psalm 98

EPIPHANY

The Epiphany A, B, C	Psalm 72
First Sunday after the Epiphany/Baptism of the Lord A, B, C	Psalm 29
Second Sunday after the Epiphany B	Psalm 67
Fourth Sunday after the Epiphany A, B	Psalm 1
Sixth Sunday after the Epiphany C	Psalm 1
Seventh Sunday after the Epiphany A	Psalm 103
Eighth Sunday after the Epiphany B	Psalm 103
Last Sunday after the Epiphany/Transfiguration A	Psalm 2

LENT

Ash Wednesday A, B, C	Psalm 51
First Sunday in Lent A	Psalm 130
First Sunday in Lent C	Psalm 91
Third Sunday in Lent A	Psalm 95
Third Sunday in Lent B	Psalm 19
Third Sunday in Lent C	Psalm 103
Fourth Sunday in Lent A	Psalm 23
Fourth Sunday in Lent B	Psalm 137
Fifth Sunday in Lent B	Psalm 51

EASTER

Easter Vigil A, B, C	Psalm 98
Second Sunday of Easter B	Psalm 148
Third Sunday of Easter B	Psalm 139
Fourth Sunday of Easter A, B	Psalm 23

Fourth Sunday of Easter C	Psalm 100
Sixth Sunday of Easter B	Psalm 98
Sixth Sunday of Easter C	Psalm 67
Seventh Sunday of Easter A, B, C	Psalm 47

PENTECOST

First Sunday after Pentecost/Trinity Sunday A	Psalm 150
First Sunday after Pentecost/Trinity Sunday C	Psalm 8
Sunday between June 12 & 18, Inclusive, A (if after Trinity Sunday)	Psalm 100
Sunday between June 19 & 25, Inclusive, C (if after Trinity Sunday)	Psalm 63
Sunday between July 17 & 23, Inclusive, B	Psalm 23
Sunday between August 14 & 20, Inclusive, A	Psalm 67
Sunday between September 11 & 17, Inclusive, A	Psalm 103
Sunday between September 11 & 17, Inclusive, C	Psalm 51
Sunday between October 2 & 8, Inclusive, C	Psalm 95
Sunday between October 9 & 15, Inclusive, A	Psalm 23
Sunday between October 16 & 22, Inclusive, C	Psalm 121
Sunday between October 23 & 29, Inclusive, B	Psalm 126
Sunday between November 6 & 12, Inclusive, A	Psalm 63
Sunday between November 13 & 19, Inclusive, C	Psalm 98
Last Sunday after Pentecost/Christ the King A	Psalm 95
Last Sunday after Pentecost/Christ the King C	Psalm 46

ALL SAINTS' DAY

All Saints' Day A, B	Psalm 24

DAILY PRAYER

Morning Prayer	Psalm 63
Evening Prayer	Psalm 141

Psalms for Singing

Musical Settings of Psalms
for
Congregation

PSALM 1

ANTIPHON

Hap-py are those who de-light in the Word of the Lord.

a b

a Happy are those who reject evil counsel,
a Who do not approve of the conduct of sinners,
  b Who do not sit among those who mock God.
a Instead, the Lord's teaching so delights them
a They ponder it day and night,
  b Becoming like trees transplanted near water.
a They bear fruit in season;
a Their leaves do not wither,
  b And all that they do turns out well.   ANTIPHON

c d

c Not so the guilty!
  d They are like wind-scattered husks.
c They will not last through the judgment;
  d The righteous assembly will not include sinners.
c The Lord approves of the deeds of the just,
  d But an evil life leads only to ruin.   ANTIPHON

Songs of Zion, no. 35
ANTIPHON: Jane Marshall
VERSE: David Goodrich and Jane Marshall
©1984 by The Upper Room

Fourth Sunday after the Epiphany A, B
Sixth Sunday after the Epiphany C

PSALM 2

ANTIPHON

All who trust in the Lord will be blessed.

a   b   c   d   e

a Why do the nations conspire,
b The peoples grumble in vain,
c The kings of the world take a stand
d And the tyrants assemble together
e Against the Lord's anointed king?   ANTIPHON

a "Let us tear off his bonds,
b And hurl from ourselves his reins!"
c Enthroned in the sky, God laughs;
d The Lord scornfully mocks them —
a Then speaks to them in wrath,
b And terrifying anger:
c "I have anointed my king,
d On Zion, my holy mountain
e I, God, declare my decree."   ANTIPHON

a The Lord said to me, "You are my son;
b Today I give birth to you.
c Ask me — I give you the nations;
d The world's farthest regions are yours.
c With an iron staff you will break them;
e You smash them like jars of clay."   ANTIPHON

a And now, you kings, pay attention;
b Earth's rulers, listen to reason.
c Serve the Lord in fear,
d And kiss God's feet in terror.
a God's anger, so easily kindled,
c Will make you wandering beggars.
e But all who trust in the Lord will be blessed.   ANTIPHON

ANTIPHON: John Erickson
VERSE: Elise Eslinger

Last Sunday of the Epiphany/Transfiguration A

SALMO 8

ANTÍFONA

Cuán glo - rio - so es Tu nom - bre, Señ - or, en to - da la tie - rra!

Más a - llá de los cie - los Te a - do - ra - ré, Aun-que a-la - be co - mo ni - ño pe-

ANTÍFONA

que - ño. For - ta - le - za for - mas - te en con - tra del re - bel - de, pues, ¡pa - ra ce - sar los ya!

Cuan - do ve - o el cie - lo que Tú has for - ma - do, La

lu - na y es - tre - llas que pu - sis - te en él, yo pre - gun - to, ¿Qué so - mos, los

ANTÍFONA

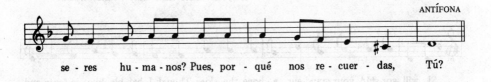

se - res hu - ma - nos? Pues, por - qué nos re - cuer - das, Tú?

ANTÍFONA: Bárbara P. García
ESTROFA: Bárbara P. García
© 1984 by The Upper Room

Domingo de la Trinidad

23

Co - mo fué - ra - mos un dios nos has cre - a - do, Señ - or. Nos ro -

deas - te de glo - ria y dig - ni - dad. So - bre to - das Tus o - bras nos

dis - te se - ño - rí - o; nos pu - sis - te por en - ci - ma de to - do.

Las o - ve - jas y bue - yes, a - ni - ma - les sal - va - jes to - dos. Las a - ves del

ANTÍFONA

cie - lo y pe - ces del mar, so - bre to - do lo que pa - se por ca - mi - nos del mar.

PSALM 8

ANTIPHON

Lord, our Lord, how splen - did is your name in all the world!

I will wor - ship your grand - eur a - bove the skies, Though I bab - ble like in - fants and

ANTIPHON: Bárbara García
VERSE: Bárbara García

©1984 by The Upper Room

First Sunday after Pentecost/ Trinity Sunday C

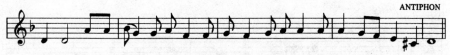

ANTIPHON

chil-dren, You have built a for-tress a-gainst your op-pon-ents, To stop the a-veng-ing foes.

When I look at the sky, the work of your fin-gers, The moon and stars you se-cured in

ANTIPHON

place, Why do you consider mere mor-tals, At-tend-ing to us, who are on-ly hu-man?

You make us lack lit - tle com-pared with your-self! You crown us with glo-ry and grand-eur.

You make us rule your oth - er crea-tures; You put ev - ry-thing un-der our feet.

All sheep and cat - tle, And e - ven wild crea-tures, The birds of the

ANTIPHON

sky and the fish of the sea; What - ev - er tra - ver - ses the paths of the sea.

25

PSALM 19

Day   and night   are   de - clar - ing God's   glo - ry;

day   and   night   are   de - clar - ing   God's glo - ry.

a   b

a The skies are declaring God's glory,
   b The firmament tells of the work of God's hands.
a Day bubbles forth speech to day,
   b And night proclaims knowledge to night;
a Without speech, without words — their voice is not heard —
   b Their call goes out to all places,
   b Their news to the ends of the world.   ANTIPHON

a There God pitched a tent for the sun —
   b Like a bridegroom leaving his chamber,
a Like a hero eager to run a race,
   b The sun comes from the end of the skies,
a And goes round to their farthest limits,
   b And nothing can hide from its heat.   ANTIPHON

ANTIPHON: David Goodrich
VERSE: Jane Marshall

© 1984 by The Upper Room

Third Sunday in Lent B

c The Lord's instruction is perfect,
  b Renewing life.
c The Lord's command can be trusted,
  b Making simple folk wise.
c The Lord's directions are true;
  b They gladden the mind.
c The Lord's decree is bright,
  b Giving light to the eyes.
c The fear of the Lord is pure;
  b It stands forever.
c The Lord's verdicts are right;
  b They are utterly just.
c Are they not more precious than gold,
  b Than much fine gold?
c And are they not sweeter than honey,
  b Than honey in combs?
c Indeed your servant takes warning from them;
  b There is great reward in keeping them. ANTIPHON

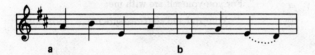

a Can anyone see their own errors?
  b Keep me free from secrets!
a In humility let me serve you;
  b Do not let my pride govern me!
a Then I shall be blameless,
  b And free from any great wrong. ANTIPHON

a May you be pleased by the words of my mouth;
  b May you be in my mind's meditations,
  b O Lord, my rock and redeemer. ANTIPHON

PSALM 23

a Lord, my shepherd, there's nothing I lack.
b In fresh pastures you let me lie down;
a You lead me beside quiet waters;
b You restore me to life. ANTIPHON

a In order to show who you are,
b You guide me in paths that are right,
a Even walking through dark valleys,
b I have no fear of harm.
a For you yourself are with me;
b Your rod and staff reassure me. ANTIPHON

a Right in front of my foes,
b You lay out a feast for me.
a You anoint my head with oil,
b My cup is overflowing. ANTIPHON

a Goodness and love pursue me
b Every day of my life;
a God's house will be my home
b As long as I may live. ANTIPHON

ANTIPHON: Jane Marshall
VERSE: Jane Marshall

©1984 by The Upper Room

Fourth Sunday in Lent A
Fourth Sunday of Easter A, B
Sunday between July 17 and 23, Inclusive, B
Sunday between October 9 and 15, Inclusive, A

PSALM 24

Who can stand in your pres - ence, O Lord?

ALTERNATE ANTIPHON

The Lord of pow - er and might, the Lord is the King of Glo - ry.

a   b

a The earth and its fullness belong to the Lord,
  b The world and all its inhabitants.

a God laid its foundations upon the seas;
  b Over cosmic rivers God made it stand firm.

a Who can go up to the Lord's own mountain?
  b Who can stand in God's holy place?

a Those whose hands have done no wrong,
  b And those whose motives are pure;

a Who do not live by deceit,
  b Or take oaths intending to break them.

a They will receive the Lord's blessing;
  b Their savior God will declare them guiltless.

a Their whole generation will search for you,
  b And seek your presence, O God of Jacob.   ANTIPHON

Hymns from the Four Winds, no. 5
Songs of Zion, no. 209
Supplement to the Book of Hymns, no. 963

ANTIPHON: Jane Marshall
ALTERNATE ANTIPHON: David Goodrich
VERSE: Jane Marshall

©1984 by The Upper Room

Fourth Sunday in Advent A
All Saints' Day A, B

a Lift up your heads, despondent gates;
 b You ancient towers, stand tall!
a The glorious king is coming.
 b Who is this glorious king?
a The Lord, with heroic strength;
 b The Lord, heroic in war.
a Lift up your heads, despondent gates;
 b You ancient towers, stand tall!
a The glorious king is coming.
 b Who is this glorious king?
a The Lord of the armies of earth and sky —
 b God is the glorious king.   ANTIPHON

PSALM 29

ANTIPHON

In splen - dor and pow'r God's glo - ry ap - pears.

a   b

a Give to the Lord, you creatures of heaven,
  b Give to the Lord all glory and power.
a Give to the Lord a glorious name;
  b Bow down to the Lord in holy splendor.   ANTIPHON

a The voice of the Lord sounds over the oceans —
  b Crashing thunder above the deep seas.
a The voice of the Lord is power;
  b The voice of the Lord is splendor.
a The voice of the Lord splits the cedars;
  b God splinters the cedars of Lebanon.
a God makes Lebanon skip like a calf,
  b Mount Hermon skip like a wild young ox.   ANTIPHON

a Slashing the sky with lightning-swords,
a The Lord's voice makes the desert writhe;
  b The desert of Kadesh quakes.
a In terror, the deer flee God's thunder,
a That snaps the limbs from the trees;
  b In the temple God's glory appears!   ANTIPHON

a The throne of the Lord is above sky and sea;
  b The Lord will rule forever.
a Lord, give strength to your people;
  b Lord, bless your people with peace.   ANTIPHON

Hymns from the Four Winds, no. 9   First Sunday after the Epiphany/ Baptism of the Lord A, B, C
ANTIPHON: Jane Marshall
VERSE: John Erickson

PSALM 46

ANTIPHON

The Lord of the arm-ies of earth and sky,

The God of Ja-cob our for-tress is with us!

ALTERNATE ANTIPHON

The migh-ty Lord is with us, the God of Ja-cob is our for-tress.

a   b   c   d

   a God is our safety and power;
     b We find great help in disaster.
       c We will not fear if the earth should change,
         d If the mountains fall to the depths of the sea,
       c If the oceans roar and foam,
         d If the mountains topple into the valleys.   ANTIPHON

   a Deep cosmic rivers delight God's city,
     b The hallowed home of God most high.
       c God is within her; she will not totter.
       d God will help her long before dawn.
       c The nations riot; the kingdoms reel —
        d God cries out, and the earth is shaken.   ANTIPHON

   a Come, see the deeds of the Lord,
     b Who sends to earth desolation —
       c Stopping wars in the world's farthest regions —
        d Weapons are shattered, wagons are burned.
       c "Enough! Admit that I am God,
        d High over the nations, high over the world."   ANTIPHON

ANTIPHON: Elise Eslinger
ALTERNATE ANTIPHON: Jane Marshall
VERSE: Jane Marshall

Last Sunday after Pentecost/ Christ the King C

© 1984 by The Upper Room

PSALM 47

ANTIPHON

Let all na-tions clap their hands; God rules o-ver all the world.

a Let all nations clap their hands;
 b Let all gods shout with laughter.
a For the Lord on high is fearful,
 b A great king over all the gods,
a Making nations submit to us,
 b Putting peoples under our feet,
a Choosing for us our heritage,
 b Jacob's proud land, beloved by God.
a God ascends with a shout!
 b The Lord, with a trumpet-blast!   ANTIPHON

c Sing, you gods, sing out!
 d Sing to our king, sing out!
c For God rules over all the world;
 d Sing a song, all you gods.
c God rules over the nations;
 d God sits on the holy throne.
c The leaders of nations are gathered,
 d With us the people of Abraham's God.
c For to God belong the world's rulers;
 d God is exalted on high.   ANTIPHON

ANTIPHON: Jane Marshall
VERSE: Jane Marshall

© 1984 by The Upper Room

Seventh Sunday of Easter A, B, C

33

PSALM 51

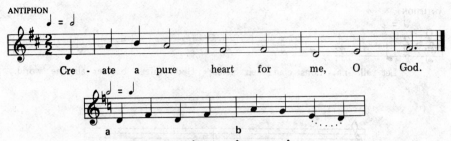

ANTIPHON

Cre - ate a pure heart for me, O God.

a   b

a God, in your mercy be gracious to me;
 b In your great compassion erase my rebellion.

a Cleanse me from guilt, again and again,
 b And purify me from my sin.

a For too well do I know my rebellion,
 b I am always aware of my sin;

a Against you alone have I sinned,
 b I have done what you despise.

a So you are right in your decree;
 b So you are blameless in judgment.

a Perverse I have been since I was conceived,
 b A sinner since my mother bore me.

a Truth, not learning, is what you desire,
 b Wisdom, not craft, is what you teach me.   ANTIPHON

c   d

c Make me cleaner than fresh-flowing water;
 d Wash me and I will be whiter than snow.

c Invite me to joyous delight,
 d Let the bones you have broken rejoice.

c Hide your face from my sin,
 d And wipe away all my guilt.

c Create a pure heart for me, O God;
 d Renew within me a steady spirit.

c Do not throw me out of your presence;
 d Nor take your holy spirit from me.

Songs of Zion, no. 182
ANTIPHON: Jane Marshall
VERSE: Jane Marshall
©1984 by The Upper Room

Ash Wednesday A, B, C
Fifth Sunday in Lent B
Sunday between September 11 and 17, Inclusive, C

c Bring back to me your joyous salvation,
  d Let your spirit freely support me;
c Let me teach your ways to rebels,
  d Let sinners return to you.   ANTIPHON

a Save me, O God, from deadly guilt;
  b My tongue will shout out your justice.
a Lord, may you open my lips,
  b And my mouth will declare your praise.
a I would sacrifice if you wanted;
  b You are not pleased with burnt offerings.
a God, my gift is a broken will;
  b You do not scorn a submissive heart.   ANTIPHON

PSALM 63

In the shade of your wings I shout for joy.

ALTERNATE ANTIPHON

Be - cause your grace is bet - ter than life my lips will praise you.

a   b

a O God, my God, I am eager to find you;
b My heart is thirsty for you.
a In my weakness I yearn for you,
b As though in a dry and weary land.
a I look in your holy place for you,
b To see your strength and glory. ANTIPHON

c   d

c Because your grace is better than life,
d My lips will praise you.
c As long as I live, I will bless you;
d I lift up my hands in your name.
c I am filled as though with the finest foods,
d And with joyful lips I praise you.
c In my bed, remembering you,
d I ponder you in the darkness.
c It is you who come to my aid;
d In the shade of your wings I shout for joy. ANTIPHON

Hymns from the Four Winds, no. 80
Songs of Zion, no. 179

ANTIPHON: Jane Marshall
ALTERNATE ANTIPHON: John Erickson
VERSE: Jane Marshall

©1984 by The Upper Room

Sunday between June 19 and 25, Inclusive, C
(if after Trinity Sunday)
Sunday between November 6 and 12, Inclusive, A
Daily Morning Prayer

a My inmost self pursues you,
  b Your right hand holds me fast.
a Some people are trying to trap me,
  b But they will be sent to the grave;
a The sword will spill their blood,
  b And they will be jackals' food.
a And our king will rejoice in God;
  b His faithful subjects will triumph,
a And God will shut the mouths
  b Of those who go on telling lies.   ANTIPHON

PSALM 67

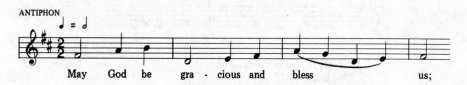

ANTIPHON

May God be gra - cious and bless us;

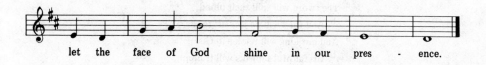

let the face of God shine in our pres - ence.

a   b   c   d

 a Knowing your way on the earth,
   b Your saving work in all countries,
      c The peoples will praise you, God;
         d The peoples all will praise you.
 a Nations will shout and rejoice,
   b For you rule the peoples fairly,
         d And guide the nations on earth.   ANTIPHON

 a The peoples will praise you, God;
   b The peoples all will praise you.
      c Let the earth yield her produce;
         d Let God, our God, now bless us.
 a Bless us; you are our God!
   b Then we will worship you
         d In all the world's farthest regions.   ANTIPHON

ANTIPHON: Jane Marshall
VERSE: Elise Eslinger

© 1984 by The Upper Room

Second Sunday after the Epiphany B
Sixth Sunday of Easter C
Sunday between August 14 and 20, Inclusive, A

PSALM 72

ANTIPHON

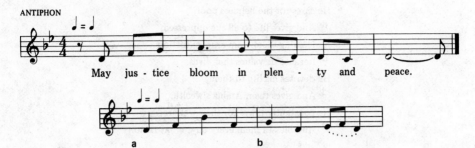

May jus - tice bloom in plen - ty and peace.

a

b

a O God, let the king be righteous;
  b Let the heir to the throne be just.

a Let him plead the cause of your people;
  b Let the poor obtain true justice.

a Let mountains declare, "God's people are innocent!"
  b And the hills, "We are setting them free!"

a May he help the oppressed find justice,
  b Save the poor, and crush the exploiter.

a Let him outlive the sun and the moon,
  b Through all generations to come.

a Let him fall like rain on the grass,
  b Like showers sprinkling the earth.   ANTIPHON

c

d

c Throughout his reign let justice bloom
  d In plenty and peace, while the moon endures.

c Let him be king from sea to sea,
  d From the river Euphrates to earth's farthest end.

c Let his enemies kneel before him;
  d Let his foes all lick the dust.

c Let kings to the north and west bring tribute;
  d Let kings to the south and east bring gifts.

c Let all the kings bow before him;
  d Let all the nations serve him.

c For he saves the poor when they cry for help,
  d The oppressed when no one will aid them.

ANTIPHON: Judy Loehr
VERSE: Jane Marshall

Second Sunday in Advent A
The Epiphany A, B, C

^c He cares for the helpless poor,

   ^d And gives life to all the oppressed,

^c Redeeming them from cruel extortion

   ^d Because he values their lives.

^c He devotes his life to them,

   ^d And gives them Arabia's wealth.

^c He constantly prays for their welfare,

   ^d And blesses them every day.   ANTIPHON

^a Let grain abound in the land,

   ^b Let it wave on the mountaintops!

^a Let the harvest bloom as in Lebanon,

   ^b In the cities as much as the fields!

^a Let his name live forever,

   ^b Let his descendants outshine the sun.

^a Let all nations seek his blessing,

   ^b And find themselves blessed in him.   ANTIPHON

PSALM 91

ANTIPHON

The Lord is your (our) re - fuge, the most high your (our) shel - ter.

a You live in God's secret place;
b The Most High shades your sleep.

a You say to the Lord, "My strong refuge,
b My God, in whom I trust."

a God saves you from fowlers' snares,
b And from deadly disease.

a The Lord's pinions are over you;
b You hide beneath God's wings. ANTIPHON

c Do not fear the terror of night,
d Or the arrow that flies by day,

c The pestilence stalking in darkness,
d The plague laying waste at noon.

c A thousand may fall at your side,
d Ten thousand at your right hand;

c But you will not be stricken —
d The faithful God is your shield and tower.

c Only look with your eyes,
d And see the oppressors punished.

c As for you, the Lord is your refuge;
d You have made the Most High your shelter.

c Evil will not befall you,
d Nor harm approach your tent.

c On your behalf, God commanded the angels
d To guard you in all your ways.

c Their hands will lift you high,
d Lest you catch your foot on a stone.

c You shall step on lion and snake,
d Tread down young lion and serpent. ANTIPHON

ANTIPHON: Elise Eslinger
VERSE: Jane Marshall

© 1984 by The Upper Room

First Sunday in Lent C

a "I will save those who cling to me,
 b And protect those who know my name.
a They call and I answer them;
 b I am with them in their distress.
a I will rescue them and reward them;
 b I satisfy them with long life,
 b And show them my saving power." ANTIPHON

PSALM 95

Come, let us sing to the Lord; let us shout to our sav - ing Rock!

a   b

a Come, let us sing to the Lord;
  b Let us shout to our saving Rock!

a Enter God's presence with praise,
  b With music and shouts of joy.

a For the Lord is a mighty God,
  b The great ruler of all the gods.

a God's hand holds the depths of the world,
  b And rules the peaks of the mountains.

a It is God who made and rules the seas,
  b Whose hand created dry ground.

a Come, let us kneel and worship the Lord;
  b Let us bow before God our maker.   ANTIPHON

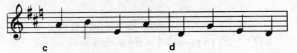

c   d

c Today God will be our God —
  d Who chooses a people and tends them,

c Whose hand will guide us like sheep —
  d If you will only heed God's voice;

c "Do not harden your hearts as you did at Meribah —
  d As you did at Massah in the desert.

c There your ancestors put me on trial;
  d Having seen my power, they tested me still!

c For forty years I despised them all —
  d I saw how weak-willed they were.

c Because they ignored my ways,
  d I swore in my anger to give them no rest."   ANTIPHON

ANTIPHON: Jane Marshall
VERSE: Jane Marshall

Third Sunday in Lent A
Sunday between October 2 and 8, Inclusive, C
Last Sunday after Pentecost/ Christ the King A

PSALM 98

Sing a new song to the Lord, who has done such mar-vel-ous things.

ALTERNATE ANTIPHON

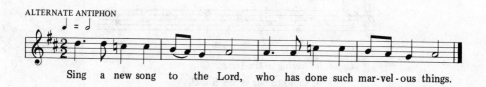

Sing a new song to the Lord, who has done such mar-vel-ous things.

a   b

a Sing a new song to the Lord,
   b Who has done such marvelous things,
a Whose right hand and holy arm
   b Have come to rescue me.   ANTIPHON

a Lord, you made known your saving power;
   b You revealed to the nations your justice.
a You remembered your faithful love,
   b For all your family Israel.
a The farthest ends of the world
   b Have seen our God's saving power.   ANTIPHON

a Shout to the Lord, every land!
   b Be confident! Shout and sing!
a Sing to the Lord with a harp,
   b With a harp and the sound of music!
a With sounding horns and trumpets,
   b Shout to the Lord, the King!   ANTIPHON

Celebremos, no. 11

ANTIPHON: Jane Marshall
ALTERNATE ANTIPHON: David Goodrich
VERSE: Jane Marshall

© 1984 by The Upper Room

Christmas Eve/Day B
Easter Vigil A, B, C
Sixth Sunday of Easter B
Sunday between November 13 and 19, Inclusive, C

a Storm, you ocean, and all that fills you,
 b You lands, and all who inhabit you.
a Clap your hands, great rivers;
 b You hills, all shout together
a Before the Lord, who comes,
 b Who comes to rule the world,
a To rule the lands with justice
 b And rightly govern the peoples.   ANTIPHON

PSALM 100

ANTIPHON

En - ter God's gates with thanks and praise.

VERSE

Shout to the Lord, all the land; Serve the Lord with joy;

Come be-fore God with laugh - ter. Know that the Lord is God;

We be - long to the Lord our Ma - ker, To

God, who tends us like sheep. Come to God's gates with

thanks; Come to God's courts with praise;

Praise and bless the Lord's name. Tru - ly the Lord is good;

God is al - ways gra - cious, And faith - ful age af - ter - age. ANTIPHON

Hymns from the Four Winds, no. 18, no. 45
ANTIPHON: J. Jefferson Cleveland
VERSE: J. Jefferson Cleveland
©1984 by The Upper Room

Fourth Sunday of Easter C
Sunday between June 12 and 18, Inclusive, A
(if after Trinity Sunday)

PSALM 103

ANTIPHON

Bless the Lord my in-most self, Bless God's Ho-ly name.

ALTERNATE ANTIPHON

Com - pas - sion and grace— that is the Lord.

a   b

a Bless the Lord, my inmost self!

  b Everything in me, bless God's holy name.

a Bless the Lord, my inmost self,

  b Do not forget what God has done —

a Pardoning all your sin,

  b Healing your every disease,

a Redeeming your life from the grave,

  b Crowning your head with constant compassion.

a Your vital needs are satisfied;

  b Like the phoenix, your youth is renewed.

a The Lord accomplishes justice —

  b Vindication for all the oppressed!   ANTIPHON

c   d

c God's ways were made known to Moses,

  d God's acts to Israel's offspring.

c Compassion and grace — that is the Lord,

  d Slow to be angry, determined to love us!

ANTIPHON: David Goodrich
ALTERNATE ANTIPHON: Jane Marshall
VERSE: Jane Marshall

© 1984 by The Upper Room

Seventh Sunday after the Epiphany A
Eighth Sunday after the Epiphany B
Third Sunday in Lent C
Sunday between September 11 and 17, Inclusive, A

47

^c God will not always oppose us,
  ^d Nor hold a grudge forever.
^c God does not act in accord with our sins,
  ^d Nor as our guilt deserves.
^c As high as the sky is above the world,
  ^d So great is the grace given those who fear God.
^c As far as the east is from the west,
  ^d God removes our offences from us.
^c Like a father's love for his child
  ^d Is the love shown to those who fear God.
^c Surely God knows how we were made,
  ^d And recalls that we are dust!
^c Our human life is a reed,
  ^d A flower that blooms in the meadow.
^c It is gone when the wind blows over it;
  ^d Its place recalls it no more. ANTIPHON

a   b

^a But the grace of the Lord is eternal,
  ^b Resting forever on those who fear God.
^a God's justice belongs to their offspring,
  ^b To all who keep the covenant;
  ^b Who remember to do what God commands.
^a The Lord has set a throne in the sky;
  ^b God's authority governs all things.
^a Divine messenger, bless the Lord.
  ^b Mighty heroes, doing God's word,
  ^b And hearing the word God speaks.
^a Divine warriors, bless the Lord,
  ^b Servants who do whatever God pleases.
^a All you creatures, bless the Lord
  ^b Whose dominion is everywhere.
  ^b Bless the Lord, my inmost self! ANTIPHON

PSALM 121

ANTIPHON

My help comes from the Lord (the Ma - ker of earth and sky).

a   b

a I look at the hills, and wonder
  b From where will my help come?
a My help comes from the Lord,
  b The maker of earth and sky.
a May God not let you stumble;
  b May God your protector not sleep!
a Truly God never rests or sleeps,
  b Protecting Israel.   ANTIPHON

a The Lord is your protector,
  b The shade at your right hand.
a The sun will not strike you by day,
  b Nor the moon at night.
a The Lord protects you from every evil;
  b God protects your life.
a The Lord will protect you, coming and going,
  b Now, and forevermore.   ANTIPHON

Hymns from the Four Winds, no. 117
Songs of Zion, no. 173

ANTIPHON: Jane Marshall
VERSE: Jane Marshall

© 1984 by The Upper Room

Sunday between October 16 and 22, Inclusive, C

PSALM 126

ᵃ When the Lord shall again set Zion free —
   ᵇ Let us be as dreamers —
ᵃ Then laughter will fill our mouths,
   ᵇ And our tongues will shout for joy.
ᵃ They will say among the nations,
   ᵇ "The Lord has done great things for them!"
ᵃ May the Lord do great things for us,
   ᵇ And then may we rejoice!   ANTIPHON

ᵃ Lord, bring back our exiles,
   ᵇ Like streams to water the desert.
ᵃ Those who sow with tears —
   ᵇ May they gather the harvest with singing.
ᵃ True, they may go out weeping,
   ᵇ Bearing a pouch of seed;
ᵃ But let them return with laughter,
   ᵇ Bearing their sheaves of grain!   ANTIPHON

ANTIPHON: Jane Marshall
VERSE: David Goodrich

© 1984 by The Upper Room

Second Sunday in Advent C
Sunday between October 23 and 29, Inclusive, B

PSALM 130

ANTIPHON

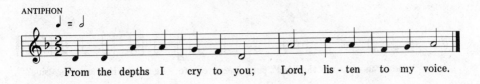

From the depths I cry to you; Lord, lis-ten to my voice.

ALTERNATE ANTIPHON

My in - most self longs for the Lord.

a   b

a From the depths I cry to you;
  b Lord, listen to my voice.
a Let your ear be open
  b To the sound of my plea for pardon.
a Lord, if you keep account of wrongs,
  b Who will be able to stand?
a But you are prepared to forgive us,
  b That we may worship you.   ANTIPHON

a My inmost self longs for the Lord;
  b I wait for the word of God.
a I tell myself, "Wait for the Lord
  b As a sentry watches for morning."
a As a sentry watches for morning,
  b Israel, wait for the Lord.
a Surely the Lord will be faithful,
  b And redeem us again and again.
a God will redeem Israel
  b From all our guilty deeds.   ANTIPHON

ANTIPHON: David Goodrich
ALTERNATE ANTIPHON: John Erickson
VERSE: Jane Marshall

© 1984 by The Upper Room

First Sunday in Lent A

PSALM 137

ANTIPHON

How can we sing the Lord's song here on for-eign soil, How can we sing?

a There by Babylon's rivers,

a We sat weeping aloud,

    b And we remembered Zion;

a On the poplars there,

    b We hung up our lyres.

a But what did they ask from us?

    b Our captors asked us to sing!

a Our tormentors cried, "Entertain us!

    b Sing to us from the songs of Zion!" ANTIPHON

a How can we sing the Lord's song,

a Here on foreign soil?

a Jerusalem, should I forget you,

    b Let my right hand shrivel;

a Let my tongue stick to my palate,

a Should I fail to remember you.

a Oh, let me go up to Jerusalem,

    b Wearing once more a festal crown! ANTIPHON

Supplement to the Book of Hymns, no. 863

Fourth Sunday in Lent B

ANTIPHON: Elise Eslinger
VERSE: Elise Eslinger

PSALM 139

Search me, O God, and know my heart. Lead me in ways that en-dure.

a

b

ᵃ Lord, you have searched and known me;

ᵇ You know my deeds and my thoughts,

ᵇ Discerning my purpose far in advance.

ᵃ You mark each digression and pause,

ᵇ Familiar with all my habits.

ᵃ There is not a word on my tongue

ᵇ Before you know it completely.

ᵃ Front and back you enclose me,

ᵇ And place your hand upon me.

ᵃ How can I comprehend such wonders,

ᵇ So far beyond my grasp!   ANTIPHON

c

b

ᶜ Where could I go, away from your Spirit?

ᵇ Where could I flee from your presence?

ᶜ If I climbed the skies, you'd be there;

ᵇ If I lay down in Hades, I'd meet you.

ᶜ If I took the wings of the dawn,

ᵇ To go live beyond the sea,

ᶜ There, too, your hand would lead me,

ᵇ Your right hand hold me fast.

ᶜ I might say, "Darkness has snatched me away;

ᵇ Night encloses me all around!"

ᶜ But darkness is not too dark for you —

ᵇ You cause the night to shine like day.   ANTIPHON

ANTIPHON: Jane Marshall
VERSE: Jane Marshall and David Goodrich

Third Sunday of Easter B

d For you created my inmost parts;

  e You wove me within my mother's womb.

d I praise you, God—how awesome you are —

  e You make me so unique, as are all your creatures!

d You have known my true self forever;

  e Nothing about me is hidden from you.

d It is you who made me in secret;

  e In the depths of the earth you knit me together.

d You foresaw each stage of my life;

  e They were all written down in your scroll.

d You kept track of all my days,

  e Before I had even appeared.

d O God, how highly you thought of me;

  e How great is the sum of your plans!

d I could no more count them than grains of sand;

  e Just let me awake, and still be with you.   ANTIPHON

f If only you would slay the wicked!

  g Make those murderers leave me alone!

f They think they are more crafty than you,

  g And use your inspirations for idle ends.

f Lord, I hate those who hate you —

  g I despise their rebellion against you!

f My hatred for them is complete;

  g I consider them personal foes.

d Explore me, God, and know my heart;

  e Test me and know my disquieting thoughts.

d Look for destructive ways in me,

  e And lead me in ways that endure.   ANTIPHON

PSALM 141

ANTIPHON

My prayers rise like in - cense,
my hands like an even - ing sac - ri - fice.

a   b

^a I call you, Lord; hurry to me!
  ^b Hear my voice when I call to you.
^a Let my prayer be incense before you,
  ^b My lifted hands an evening sacrifice.   ANTIPHON

c   d

^c Set a sentry, O Lord, at my mouth,
  ^d A guard at the door of my lips.
^c Don't let me dwell on evil thoughts,
  ^d Or carry them out in guilty deeds,
  ^d With people who do what is wrong.
^c I don't want to share their sumptuous feasts.
  ^d Let them beat me for being righteous,
  ^d Or criticize me for my faith,
^c But don't let their ointment shine on my head;
  ^d Let my prayers forever oppose their schemes.
^c Let their leaders be smashed on a rock,
  ^d And let them hear these fair words of mine!   ANTIPHON

ANTIPHON: Jane Marshall
VERSE: David Goodrich, Jane Marshall

© 1984 by The Upper Room

Daily Evening Prayer

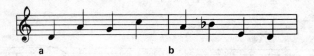

a

b

^a As though I were cut down, hacked to pieces,
^b My bones are strewn at Sheol's door.

^a Yet I look to you, Lord God;
^b I await you; don't leave me to die!

^a Save me from all their traps,
^b From the snares of those who do wrong.

^a Let the wicked fall into their own nets,
^b Then I will be able to slip away.   ANTIPHON

PSALM 148

ANTIPHON

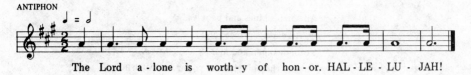

The Lord a - lone is worth-y of hon - or. HAL - LE - LU - JAH!

a   b

PRAISE THE LORD! HALLELUJAH!
a Praise God from the sky,
  b Praise God from the heights;
a Praise God, all you angels,
  b Praise God, heaven's armies.
a Praise God, sun and moon,
  b Praise God, all bright stars;
a Praise God, skies above,
  b And waters above the skies.
a They praise their true Lord,
  b Who ordered their making,
a Who placed them for ever,
  b In the courses they follow.   ANTIPHON

a   c

a Praise the Lord from the earth,
  c Ocean deeps and dragons.
a Fire and hail, snow and smoke,
  c Gale wind doing God's word;
a All mountains and hills,
  c All fruit trees and cedars,
a All beasts, wild or tame,
  c Creeping things and soaring birds;

Celebramos, no. 9
Hymns from the Four Winds, no. 3, no. 8

ANTIPHON: Jane Marshall
VERSE: Jane Marshall

© 1984 by The Upper Room

Second Sunday of Easter B

^a All earth's kings and peoples,
  ^c All earth's princes and rulers,
^a Young women and men,
  ^c And the old with the young.   ANTIPHON

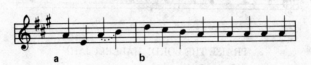

a   b

^a Praise the name of the Lord;
  ^b God alone is worthy of honor.
^a God's might is above earth and sky;
  ^b God's people rise up in power.
^a Israel's children are close to God,
  ^b God the glory of all faithful people!
PRAISE THE LORD! HALLELUJAH!   ANTIPHON

PSALM 150

a Praise God in the earthly temple;
  b Praise God in heaven's great dome.
a Praise God the mighty hero;
  b Praise God, supremely great.   ANTIPHON

a Praise God with blasting trumpets;
  b Praise God with harps and lyres.
a Praise God with drums and dancing;
  b Praise God with strings and flutes.   ANTIPHON

a Praise God with sounding cymbals;
  b Praise God with clamorous joy.
a Let all who breathe, praise the Lord.
  b Praise the Lord, Hallelujah!   ANTIPHON

ANTIPHON: David Goodrich
VERSE: David Goodrich

First Sunday after Pentecost/ Trinity Sunday A

Musical Settings of Psalms
for
Choir and Accompanist

PSALM 1

ANTIPHON

Hap - py are those who de - light in the Word of the Lord.

a Hap-py are those who re-ject evil coun-sel, a Who do not ap-prove of the

con-duct of sin-ners, b Who do not sit among those who mock God.

a In-stead, the Lord's teach-ing so de-lights them a They pon-der it day and night,

b Be-com-ing like trees trans-plant-ed near wa - ter. a They bear fruit in sea - son;

Songs of Zion, no. 35
ANTIPHON: Jane Marshall
VERSE: David Goodrich and Jane Marshall

Fourth Sunday after the Epiphany A, B
Sixth Sunday after the Epiphany C

PSALM 2

ANTIPHON: John Erickson
VERSE: Elise Eslinger

©1984 by The Upper Room

Last Sunday of the Epiphany/Transfiguration A

ANTIPHON

d The Lord scorn-fully mocks them— a Then speaks to them in wrath,

b And ter-ri-fy-ing an-ger: c "I have a-noint-ed my king,

d On Zi-on, my ho-ly moun-tain e I, God, de-clare my de-cree."

a The Lord said to me, "You are my son; b To-day I give birth to you.

c Ask me— I give you the na-tions; d The world's far-thest re-gions are yours.

66

ANTIPHON

c With an i-ron staff you will break them; e You smash them like jars of clay."

a And now, you kings, pay at-ten-tion; b Earth's rul-ers, lis-ten to rea-son.

c Serve the Lord in fear, d And kiss God's feet in ter-ror.

a God's an-ger, so eas-i-ly kin-dled, c Will make you wan-dering

ANTIPHON

beg-gars. e But all who trust in the Lord will be blessed.

SALMO 8

ANTIFONA

¡Cuán glo-rio-so es Tu nom-bre, Señ-or, en to-da la tie-rra!

Más a-llá de los cie-los Te a-do-ra-ré, Aun-que a-

la-be co-mo ni-ño pe-que-ño. For-ta-

le-za for-mas-te en con-tra del re-bel-de, pues,

ANTÍFONA

¡pa-ra ce-sar-los ya! Cuan-do ve-o el cie-lo que

ANTIFONA: Bárbara P. García
ESTROFA: Bárbara P. García

Domingo de la Trinidad

©1984 by The Upper Room

Tú has for-ma-do, La lu-na y es-tre-llas que pu-sis-te en él, yo pre-gun-to, ¿Qué so-mos, los

ANTÍFONA

se-res hu-man-os? Pues, ¿por-qué nos re-cuer-das, Tú?

Co-mo fué-ra-mos un dios nos has cre-a-do, Señ-or. Nos ro-

dea-ste de glo-ria y dig-ni-dad. So-bre to-das Tus o-bras nos

dis - te se - ño - rí - o; nos pu - sis - te por en - ci - ma de

to - do.   Las o - ve - jas y bue - yes, a - ni-

ma - les sal - va - jes to - dos. Las a - ves del cie - lo y

ANTÍFONA

pe - ces del mar, so - bre to - do lo que pa - se por ca - mi - nos del mar.

PSALM 8

ANTIPHON

Lord, our Lord, how splen-did is your name in all the world!

I will wor-ship your grand-eur a-bove the skies, Though I

bab-ble like in-fants and chil-dren, You have

built a for-tress a-gainst your op-pon-ents, To

ANTIPHON

stop the a-veng-ing foes.

ANTIPHON: Bárbara P. García
VERSE: Bárbara P. García

First Sunday after Pentecost/Trinity Sunday C

©1984 by The Upper Room

When I look at the sky, the work of your fin-gers, The
moon and stars you se-cured in place, Why do

ANTIPHON

you con-sid-er mere mor-tals, At-tend-ing to us, who are on-ly hu-man?

You make us lack lit-tle com-pared with your-self! You

crown us with glo-ry and grand-eur. You

make us rule your oth - er crea - tures; You put

ev - ry - thing un - der our feet.

All sheep and cat - tle, And e - ven wild

crea - tures, The birds of the sky and the fish of the sea; What -

ANTIPHON

ev - er tra - ver - ses the paths of the sea.

73

PSALM 19

ANTIPHON

Day and night are de-clar-ing God's glo-ry;

Day and night are de-clar-ing God's glo-ry.

a The skies are de-clar-ing God's glo-ry, b The firm-ament tells of the work of God's hands.

a Day bub-bles forth speech to day, b And night proclaims know-ledge to night;

a Without speech, without words—their voice is not heard—

ANTIPHON: David Goodrich
VERSE: Jane Marshall
© 1984 by The Upper Room

Third Sunday in Lent B

ANTIPHON

b Their call goes out to all pla - ces, b Their news to the ends of the world.

a There God pitched a tent for the sun— b Like a bride - groom leav - ing his cham - ber,

a Like a he - ro ea - ger to run a race, b The sun comes from the end of the skies,

ANTIPHON

a And goes round to their far-thest lim - its, b And noth - ing can hide from its heat.

c The Lord's in - struc - tion is per - fect, d Re - new - ing life.

75

The Lord's com-mand can be trust-ed, Making sim-ple folk wise. The Lord's di-rec-

tions are true; They glad-den the mind. The Lord's de-cree is bright,

Giv-ing light to the eyes. The fear of the Lord is pure; It stands for-

ev - er. The Lord's ver-dicts are right; They are ut - ter - ly just.

Are they not more pre-cious than gold, Than much fine gold?

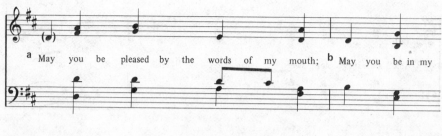

a May you be pleased by the words of my mouth; b May you be in my

mind's med - i - ta - tions, b O Lord, my rock and re - deem - er.

ANTIPHON

PSALM 23

ANTIPHON

Your good - ness and love pur - sue me, my shep - herd, my Lord.

a Lord, my shep-herd, there's noth - ing I lack. b In fresh pas-tures you let me lie down;

ANTIPHON: Jane Marshall
VERSE: Jane Marshall

©1984 by The Upper Room

Fourth Sunday in Lent A
Fourth Sunday of Easter A, B
Sunday between July 17 and 23, Inclusive, B
Sunday between October 9 and 15, Inclusive, A

ANTIPHON

a You lead me be-side quiet wa-ters; b You re-store me to life.

a In or-der to show who you are, b You guide me in paths that are right,

a E-ven walk-ing through dark val-leys, b I have no fear of harm.

ANTIPHON

a For you your-self are with me; b Your rod and staff reas-sure me.

PSALM 24

Who can stand in your pre-sence, O Lord?

The Lord of pow-er and might, the Lord is the King of Glo-ry.

a The earth and its full-ness be-long to the Lord, b The world and all its in-hab-i-tants.

a God laid its foun-da-tions up-on the seas; b Over cos-mic riv-ers God made it stand firm.

a Who can go up to the Lord's own moun-tain? b Who can stand in God's ho-ly place?

Hymns from the Four Winds, no. 5
Songs of Zion, no. 209
Supplement to the Book of Hymns, no. 963

Fourth Sunday in Advent A
All Saints' Day A, B

ANTIPHON: Jane Marshall
ALTERNATE ANTIPHON: David Goodrich
VERSE: Jane Marshall

a Those whose hands have done no wrong, b And those whose mo-tives are pure;

a Who do not live by de-ceit, b Or take oaths in-tend-ing to break them.

a They will re-ceive the Lord's bless-ing; b Their sav-ior God will de-clare them guilt-less.

ANTIPHON

a Their whole gen-er-a-tion will search for you, b And seek your pre-sence, O God of Ja-cob.

a Lift up your heads, de-spond-ent gates; b You an-cient tow-ers, stand tall!

ANTIPHON

PSALM 29

Hymns from the Four Winds, no. 9

First Sunday after the Epiphany/Baptism of the Lord A, B, C

ANTIPHON: Jane Marshall
VERSE: John Erickson

©1984 by The Upper Room

a The voice of the Lord splits the ce-dars; b God splin-ters the cedars of Le-ba-non.

ANTIPHON

a God makes Le-banon skip like a calf, b Mount Her-mon skip like a wild young ox.

a Slash-ing the sky with light-ning swords, a The Lord's voice makes the des-ert writhe;

b The desert of Ka-desh quakes. a In ter-ror, the deer flee God's thun-der,

ANTIPHON

a That snaps the limbs from the trees; b In the tem-ple God's glo-ry ap-pears!

a The throne of the Lord is a-bove sky and sea; b The Lord will rule for-ev - er.

ANTIPHON

a Lord, give strength to your peo-ple; b Lord, bless your peo-ple with peace.

PSALM 46

ANTIPHON

The Lord of the ar - mies of earth and sky, The

God of Ja - cob our for - tress is with us!

ANTIPHON: Elise Eslinger
ALTERNATE ANTIPHON: Jane Marshall
VERSE: Jane Marshall

Last Sunday after Pentecost/Christ the King C

©1984 by The Upper Room

ALTERNATE ANTIPHON

The migh-ty Lord is with us, the God of Ja-cob is our for-tress.

a God is our safe-ty and pow-er; **b** We find great help in dis-as-ter. **c** We will not fear if the earth should change, **d** If the moun-tains fall to the depths of the sea,

ANTIPHON

c If the o-ceans roar and foam, **d** If the moun-tains top-ple in-to the val-leys.

a Deep cosmic riv-ers de-light God's ci-ty, **b** The hal-lowed home of God most high.

87

c God is with-in her; she will not tot-ter. d God will help her long be-fore dawn.

ANTIPHON

c The na-tions ri-ot; the king-doms reel— d God cries out, and the earth is sha-ken.

a Come, see the deeds of the Lord, b Who sends to earth des-o-la-tion—

c Stop-ping wars in the world's far-thest re-gions— d Wea-pons are shat-tered, wag-ons are burned.

ANTIPHON

c "E-nough! Ad-mit that I am God, d High o-ver the na-tions, high o-ver the world."

88

PSALM 47

ANTIPHON

Let all nations clap their hands; God rules over all the world.

a Let all nations clap their hands; b Let all gods shout with laughter. a For the Lord on high is fearful, b A great king over all the gods, a Making nations submit to us, b Putting peoples under our feet, a Choosing for us our heritage, b Jacob's proud land, beloved by God. a God ascends with a shout! b The Lord, with a trumpet-blast!

ANTIPHON

ANTIPHON: Jane Marshall
VERSE: Jane Marshall

© 1984 by The Upper Room

Seventh Sunday of Easter A, B, C

89

c Sing, you gods, sing out! d Sing to our king, sing out!

c For God rules over all the world; d Sing a song, all you gods.

c God rules o-ver the na - tions; d God sits on the ho - ly throne.

c The lead-ers of na-tions are gath - ered, d With us the peo-ple of A-bra-ham's God.

ANTIPHON

c For to God be - long the world's rul - ers; d God is ex-alt-ed on high.

PSALM 51

ANTIPHON

Cre-ate a pure heart for me, O God.

a God, in your mer-cy be gra-cious to me; b In your great com-pas-sion e-rase my re-bellion.

a Cleanse me from guilt, a-gain and a-gain, b And pu-ri-fy me from my sin.

a For too well do I know my re-bellion, b I am al-ways a-ware of my sin;

a A-gainst you a-lone have I sinned, b I have done what you de-spise.

Songs of Zion, no. 182
ANTIPHON: Jane Marshall
VERSE: Jane Marshall

Ash Wednesday A, B, C
Fifth Sunday in Lent B
Sunday between September 11 and 17, Inclusive, C

a So you are right in your de-cree; b So you are blameless in judg-ment.

a Per-verse I have been since I was con-ceived, b A sin-ner since my moth-er bore me.

ANTIPHON

a Truth, not learn-ing, is what you de-sire, b Wis-dom, not craft, is what you teach me.

c Make me clean-er than fresh-flowing wa-ter; d Wash me and I will be whit-er than snow.

c In-vite me to joy-ous de-light, d Let the bones you have bro-ken re-joice.

c Hide your face from my sin, d And wipe a-way all my guilt.

c Cre-ate a pure heart for me, O God; d Re-new with-in me a stead-y spir-it.

c Do not throw me out of your pres-ence; d Nor take your ho-ly spir - it from me.

c Bring back to me your joy-ous sal-va-tion, d Let your spir-it free-ly sup-port me;

ANTIPHON

c Let me teach your ways to re-bels, d Let sin-ners re-turn to you.

a Save me, O God, from dead-ly guilt; b My tongue will shout out your jus-tice.

a Lord, may you o-pen my lips, b And my mouth will de-clare your praise.

a I would sac-ri-fice if you want-ed; b You are not pleased with burnt of-fer-ings.

ANTIPHON

a God, my gift is a bro-ken will; b You do not scorn a sub-missive heart.

PSALM 63

ANTIPHON

In the shade of your wings I shout for joy.

ALTERNATE ANTIPHON

Be - cause your grace is bet - ter than life my lips will praise you.

a O God, my God, I am ea - ger to find you; **b** My heart is thirs - ty for you.

a In my weak - ness I yearn for you, **b** As though in a dry and wea - ry land.

ANTIPHON

a I look in your ho - ly place for you, **b** To see your strength and glo - ry.

Hymns from the Four Winds, no. 80
Songs of Zion, no. 179

ANTIPHON: Jane Marshall
ALTERNATE ANTIPHON: John Erickson
VERSE: Jane Marshall

© 1984 by The Upper Room

Sunday between June 19 and 25, Inclusive, C
  (if after Trinity Sunday)
Sunday between November 6 and 12, Inclusive, A
Daily Morning Prayer

95

c Be - cause your grace is bet - ter than life, d My lips will praise you.

c As long as I live, I will bless you; d I lift up my hands in your name.

c I am filled as though with the fin - est foods, d And with joy - ful lips I praise you.

c In my bed, re - mem - ber - ing you, d I pon - der you in the dark - ness.

ANTIPHON

c It is you who come to my aid; d In the shade of your wings I shout for joy.

a My in-most self pur-sues you, b Your right hand holds me fast.

a Some peo-ple are try-ing to trap me, b But they will be sent to the grave;

a The sword will spill their blood, b And they will be jack-als' food.

a And our king will re-joice in God; b His faith-ful sub-jects will tri-umph,

ANTIPHON

a And God will shut the mouths b Of those who go on tell-ing lies.

PSALM 67

May God be gra - cious and bless us;
let the face of God shine in our pre - sence.

a Know-ing your way on the earth, **b** your sav-ing work in all coun-tries, **c** The peo - ples will praise you, God; **d** The peo-ples all will praise you. **a** Na-tions will shout and re-joice,

ANTIPHON: Jane Marshall
VERSE: Elise Eslinger
© 1984 by The Upper Room

Second Sunday after the Epiphany B
Sixth Sunday of Easter C
Sunday between August 14 and 20, Inclusive, A

ANTIPHON

b For you rule the peo - ples fair - ly, **d** And guide the na - tions on earth.

a The peo - ples will praise you, God; **b** The peo - ples all will praise you. **c** Let the earth

yield her pro - duce; **d** Let God, our God, now bless us. **a** Bless us; you are our God!

ANTIPHON

b Then we will wor - ship you **d** In all the world's farth - est re - gions.

99

PSALM 72

ANTIPHON

May jus-tice bloom in plen-ty and peace.

a O God, let the king be right-eous; b Let the heir to the throne be just.

a Let him plead the cause of your peo-ple; b Let the poor ob-tain true jus-tice.

a Let moun-tains de-clare, "God's peo-ple are in-nocent!" b And the hills, "We are set-ting them free!"

a May he help the op-pressed find jus-tice, b Save the poor, and crush the ex-ploit-er.

ANTIPHON: Judy Loehr
VERSE: Jane Marshall
© 1984 by The Upper Room

Second Sunday in Advent A
The Epiphany A, B, C

100

a Let him out-live the sun and the moon, b Through all gen-er-a-tions to come.

ANTIPHON

a Let him fall like rain on the grass, b Like show-ers sprink-ling the earth.

c Through-out his reign let jus-tice bloom d In plen-ty and peace, while the moon en-dures.

c Let him be king from sea to sea, d From the riv-er Eu-phra-tes to earth's farth-est end.

c Let his en-emies kneel be-fore him; d Let his foes all lick the dust.

c Let kings to the north and west bring tri-bute; d Let kings to the south and east bring gifts.

c Let all the kings bow be-fore him; d Let all the na - tions serve him.

c For he saves the poor when they cry for help, d The op-pressed when no one will aid them.

c He cares for the help - less poor, d And gives life to all the op - pressed,

c Re - deem - ing them from cruel ex - tor-tion d Be - cause he val - ues their lives.

c He de - votes his life to them, d And gives them A - rab - ia's wealth.

ANTIPHON

c He con-stantly prays for their wel - fare, d And bless - es them ev -ery day.

a Let grain a - bound in the land, b Let it wave on the moun - tain - tops!

a Let the har-vest bloom as in Leb-an-on, b In the cit-ies as much as the fields!

a Let his name live for - ever, b Let his de - scen - dants out - shine the sun.

ANTIPHON

a Let all na - tions seek his bless-ing, b And find them - selves blessed in him.

PSALM 91

ANTIPHON

The Lord is your (our) re-fuge, the most high your (our) shel-ter.

a You live in God's se-cret place; b The Most High shades your sleep.

a You say to the Lord, "My strong re-fuge, b My God, in whom I trust."

a God saves you from fowl-ers' snares, b And from dead-ly dis-ease.

ANTIPHON

a The Lord's pin-ions are o-ver you; b You hide be-neath God's wings.

ANTIPHON: Elise Eslinger
VERSE: Jane Marshall
© 1984 by The Upper Room

First Sunday in Lent C

c Do not fear the ter-ror of night, **d** Or the arrow that flies by day,

c The pes-tilence stalk-ing in dark-ness, **d** The plague lay-ing waste at noon.

c A thou-sand may fall at your side, **d** Ten thou-sand at your right hand;

c But you will not be strick-en— **d** The faith-ful God is your shield and tow-er.

c On-ly look with your eyes, **d** And see the op-pres-sors pun - ished.

c As for you, the Lord is your re - fuge; **d** You have made the Most High your shel - ter.

c E - vil will not be - fall you, **d** Nor harm ap - proach your tent.

c On your be-half, God com-mand - ed the an-gels **d** To guard you in all your ways.

c Their hands will lift you high, **d** Lest you catch your foot on a stone.

ANTIPHON

c You shall step on li - on and snake, **d** Tread down young li - on and ser - pent.

ANTIPHON

PSALM 95

Come, let us sing to the Lord; let us shout to our sav - ing Rock!

a Come, let us sing to the Lord; b Let us shout to our sav - ing Rock!

a En - ter God's pre - sence with praise, b With mu - sic and shouts of joy.

a For the Lord is a might - y God, b The great rul - er of all the gods.

a God's hand holds the depths of the world, b And rules the peaks of the moun - tains.

ANTIPHON: Jane Marshall
VERSE: Jane Marshall

Third Sunday in Lent A
Sunday between October 2 and 8, Inclusive, C
Last Sunday after Pentecost/Christ the King A

a It is God who made and rules the seas, b Whose hand cre-ated dry ground.

ANTIPHON

a Come, let us kneel and wor-ship the Lord; b Let us bow before God our mak-er.

c To - day God will be our God — d Who chooses a peo-ple and tends them,

c Whose hand will guide us like sheep — d If you will on-ly heed God's voice;

c "Do not harden your hearts as you did at Me-ri-bah — d As you did at Mas-sah in the des-ert.

109

There your an-cestors put me on tri-al; Having seen my power, they test-ed me still!

For for-ty years I des-spised them all— I saw how weak-willed they were.

ANTIPHON

Be-cause they ig-nored my ways, I swore in my an-ger to give them no rest."

PSALM 98

ANTIPHON

Sing a new song to the Lord, who has done such mar-vel-ous things.

ALTERNATE ANTIPHON

Sing a new song to the Lord, who has done such mar-vel-ous things.

Celebremos, no. 11

ANTIPHON: Jane Marshall
ALTERNATE ANTIPHON: David Goodrich
VERSE: Jane Marshall

© 1984 by The Upper Room

Christmas Eve/Day B
Easter Vigil A, B, C
Sixth Sunday of Easter B
Sunday between November 13 and 19, Inclusive, C

a Sing a new song to the Lord, **b** Who has done such mar-vel-ous things,

ANTIPHON

a Whose right hand and ho-ly arm **b** Have come to res-cue me.

a Lord, you made known your sav-ing pow-er; **b** You re-vealed to the na-tions your jus-tice.

a You re-mem-bered your faith-ful love, **b** For all your fam-ily Is-ra-el.

ANTIPHON

a The far-thest ends of the world **b** Have seen our God's sav-ing pow-er.

111

a Shout to the Lord, ev - ery land! b Be con - fi - dent! Shout and sing!

a Sing to the Lord with a harp, b With a harp and the sound of mu-sic!

ANTIPHON

a With sound - ing horns and trum - pets, b Shout to the Lord, the King!

a Storm, you o-cean, and all that fills you, b You lands, and all who in - hab - it you.

a Clap your hands, great riv - ers; b You hills, all shout to - geth - er

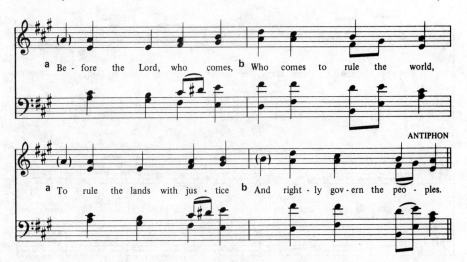

a Be - fore the Lord, who comes, b Who comes to rule the world,

ANTIPHON

a To rule the lands with jus - tice b And right - ly gov - ern the peo - ples.

PSALM 100

ANTIPHON

En - ter God's gates with thanks and praise.

Shout to the Lord, all the land; Serve the Lord with joy;

Hymns from the Four Winds, no. 18, no. 45
ANTIPHON: J. Jefferson Cleveland
VERSE: J. Jefferson Cleveland
©1984 by The Upper Room

Fourth Sunday of Easter C
Sunday between June 12 and 18, Inclusive, A
(if after Trinity Sunday)

PSALM 103

ANTIPHON

Bless the Lord my in-most self, Bless God's Ho-ly name.

ALTERNATE ANTIPHON

Com-pas-sion and grace — that is the Lord.

a Bless the Lord, my in-most self! **b** Ev-erything in me, bless God's ho-ly name.

a Bless the Lord, my in-most self, **b** Do not for-get what God has done—

a Par-doning all your sin, **b** Heal-ing your ev-ery dis-ease,

ANTIPHON: David Goodrich
ALTERNATE ANTIPHON: Jane Marshall
VERSE: Jane Marshall

© 1984 by The Upper Room

Seventh Sunday after the Epiphany A
Eighth Sunday after the Epiphany B
Third Sunday in Lent C
Sunday between September 11 and 17, Inclusive, A

115

a Re-deem-ing your life from the grave, b Crown-ing your head with con-stant com-pas-sion.

a Your vi-tal needs are sat-is-fied; b Like the phoe-nix, your youth is re - newed.

ANTIPHON

a The Lord ac-com-plishes jus-tice— b Vin-di-ca-tion for all the op-pressed!

c God's ways were made known to Mo-ses, d God's acts to Is-ra-el's off-spring.

c Com-pas-sion and grace—that is the Lord, d Slow to be an-gry, de-ter-mined to love us!

c God will not al-ways op-pose us, d Nor hold a grudge for-ev-er.

c God does not act in ac-cord with our sins, d Nor as our guilt de-serves.

c As high as the sky is a-bove the world, d So great is the grace given those who fear God.

c As far as the east is from the west, d God re-moves our of-fences from us.

c Like a fa-ther's love for his child d Is the love shown to those who fear God.

c Sure - ly God knows how we were made, d And re - calls that we are dust!

c Our hu-man life is a reed, d A flow-er that blooms in the mea - dow.

ANTIPHON

c It is gone when the wind blows o - ver it; d Its place re - calls it no more.

a But the grace of the Lord is e-ter - nal, b Rest - ing for-ev-er on those who fear God.

a God's jus-tice be-longs to their off - spring, b To all who keep the cov - e - nant;

b Who re-mem-ber to do what God com-mands. a The Lord has set a throne in the sky;

b God's au-thor-i-ty gov-erns all things. a Di-vine mes-sen-ger, bless the Lord. b Might-y her-oes,

do-ing God's word, b And hear-ing the word God speaks. a Di-vine war-riors, bless the Lord,

b Ser-vants who do what - ev-er God pleas-es. a All you crea-tures, bless the Lord

ANTIPHON

b Whose do-min-ion is ev - er-y-where. b Bless the Lord, my in - most self!

PSALM 121

ANTIPHON

My help comes from the Lord (the Ma-ker of earth and sky).

a I look at the hills, and won-der b From where will my help come?

a My help comes from the Lord, b The mak-er of earth and sky.

a May God not let you stum-ble; b May God your pro-tect-or not sleep!

Hymns from the Four Winds, no. 117
Songs of Zion, no. 173

Sunday between October 16 and 22, Inclusive, C

ANTIPHON: Jane Marshall
VERSE: Jane Marshall

ANTIPHON

a Tru-ly God never rests or sleeps, b Pro-tect-ing Is - ra - el.

a The Lord is your pro-tect - or, b The shade at your right hand.

a The sun will not strike you by day, b Nor the moon at night.

a The Lord pro-tects you from ev-ery e-vil; b God pro-tects your life.

ANTIPHON

a The Lord will pro-tect you, com-ing and go-ing, b Now, and for-ev-er - more.

121

PSALM 126

ANTIPHON

We shall re-turn with laugh-ter, sing-ing and shout-ing for joy.

a When the Lord shall a-gain set Zi-on free— b Let us be as dream-ers—

a Then laugh-ter will fill our mouths, b And our tongues will shout for joy.

a They will say a-mong the na-tions, b "The Lord has done great things for them!"

ANTIPHON: Jane Marshall
VERSE: David Goodrich
© 1984 by The Upper Room

Second Sunday in Advent C
Sunday between October 23 and 29, Inclusive, B

PSALM 130

ANTIPHON

From the depths I cry to you; Lord, lis-ten to my voice.

ALTERNATE ANTIPHON

My in-most self longs for the Lord.

a From the depths I cry to you; b Lord, lis-ten to my voice. a Let your ear be o-pen

b To the sound of my plea for par-don. a Lord, if you keep ac-count of wrongs, b Who will be

ANTIPHON

a-ble to stand? a But you are pre-pared to for-give us, b That we may wor-ship you.

ANTIPHON: David Goodrich
ALTERNATE ANTIPHON: John Erickson
VERSE: Jane Marshall

First Sunday in Lent A

a My in-most self longs for the Lord; **b** I wait for the word of God.

a I tell my-self, "Wait for the Lord **b** As a sen-try watch-es for morn - ing."

a As a sen-try watch-es for morn - ing, **b** Is-rael, wait for the Lord.

a Sure-ly the Lord will be faith - ful, **b** And re - deem us a - gain and a-gain.

ANTIPHON

a God will re - deem Is - ra - el **b** From all our guil - ty deeds.

PSALM 137

ANTIPHON

How can we sing the Lord's song here on for-eign soil, How can we sing?

a There by Baby-lon's riv-ers, **a** We sat weep-ing a-loud, **b** And we re-mem-bered Zi-on;

a On the pop-lars there, **b** We hung up our lyres.

a But what did they ask from us? **b** Our cap-tors asked us to sing!

Supplement to the Book of Hymns, no. 863

Fourth Sunday in Lent B

ANTIPHON: Elise Eslinger
VERSE: Elise Eslinger

126

PSALM 139

ANTIPHON

Search me, O God, and know my heart. Lead me in ways that en - dure.

a Lord, you have searched and known me; **b** You know my deeds and my thoughts,

b Dis-cern-ing my pur-pose far in ad-vance. **a** You mark each di-gression and pause,

b Fa-miliar with all my ha-bits. **a** There is not a word on my tongue **b** Be-fore you know it com-plete-ly.

ANTIPHON: Jane Marshall
VERSE: Jane Marshall and David Goodrich
©1984 by The Upper Room

Third Sunday of Easter B

128

a Front and back you en-close me, **b** And place your hand up-on me.

ANTIPHON

a How can I com-pre-hend such won-ders, **b** So far be-yond my grasp!

c Where could I go, a-way from your Spir-it? **b** Where could I flee from your pres-ence?

c If I climbed the skies, you'd be there; **b** If I lay down in Ha-des, I'd meet you.

129

c If I took the wings of the dawn, **b** To go live be-yond the sea,

c There, too, your hand would lead me, **b** Your right hand hold me fast.

c I might say, "Dark-ness has snatched me a-way; **b** Night en-clos-es me all a-round!"

ANTIPHON

c But dark-ness is not too dark for you—**b** You cause the night to shine like day.

d For you cre-a-ted my in-most parts; **e** You wove me with-in my moth-er's womb.

d I praise you, God—how awe-some you are— **e** You make me so u-nique, as are all your crea-tures!

d You have known my true self for-ev-er; **e** Noth-ing a-bout me is hid-den from you.

d It is you who made me in se-cret; **e** In the depths of the earth you knit me to-gether.

131

d You fore-saw each stage of my life; e They were all written down in your scroll.

d You kept track of all my days, e Be-fore I had e-ven ap-peared.

d O God, how high-ly you thought of me; e How great is the sum of your plans!

ANTIPHON

d I could no more count them than grains of sand; e Just let me a-wake, and still be with you.

f If on-ly you would slay the wick-ed! g Make those mur-derers leave me a-lone!

132

f They think they are more craft-y than you, g And use your in-spi-ra-tions for id-le ends.

f Lord, I hate those who hate you— g I de-spise their re-bel-lion a-gainst you!

f My ha-tred for them is com-plete; g I con-sid-er them per-son-al foes.

d Ex-plore me, God, and know my heart; e Test me and know my dis-qui-et-ing thoughts.

ANTIPHON

d Look for de-struc-tive ways in me, e And lead me in ways that en-dure.

133

PSALM 141

ANTIPHON: Jane Marshall
VERSE: David Goodrich, Jane Marshall

© 1984 by The Upper Room

Daily Evening Prayer

c Don't let me dwell on e-vil thoughts, d Or car-ry them out in guilt-y deeds,

d With peo-ple who do what is wrong. c I don't want to share their sump-tuous feasts.

d Let them beat me for be-ing right-eous, d Or cri-ticize me for my faith,

c But don't let their oint-ment shine on my head; d Let my prayers for-ever op-pose their schemes.

PSALM 148

The Lord a-lone is worth-y of hon-or HAL-LE-LU-JAH!

PRAISE THE LORD! HALLE-LU-JAH! ᵃ Praise God from the sky,

ᵇ Praise God from the heights; ᵃ Praise God, all you an-gels,

ᵇ Praise God, heav-en's ar-mies. ᵃ Praise God, sun and moon,

Celebremos, no. 9
Hymns from the Four Winds, no. 3, no. 8
ANTIPHON: Jane Marshall
VERSE: Jane Marshall

Second Sunday of Easter B

ANTIPHON

b Praise God, all bright stars; a Praise God, skies a-bove, b And wa-ters a-bove the skies.

a They praise their true Lord, b Who or-dered their mak - ing,

a Who placed them for ev - er, b In the courses they fol - low.

a Praise the Lord from the earth, c Ocean deeps and dra - gons. a Fire and hail, snow and smoke,

c Gale wind doing God's word; a All moun-tains and hills, c All fruit trees and cedars,

a All beasts, wild or tame, c Creeping things and soar-ing birds; a All earth's kings and peoples,

ANTIPHON

c All earth's princes and rulers, a Young wo-men and men, c And the old with the young.

a Praise the name of the Lord; b God a-lone is wor-thy of hon-or. a God's might is

a-bove earth and sky; b God's peo-ple rise up in pow-er. a Israel's chil-dren are close to God,

ANTIPHON

b God the glory of all faith - ful people! PRAISE THE LORD! HALLELUJAH!

PSALM 150

Let all who breathe praise the Lord.

Let Lord.

a Praise God in the earth-ly tem-ple; b Praise God in heav-en's great dome.

a Praise God the might-y hero; b Praise God, su-preme-ly great.

ANTIPHON

ANTIPHON: David Goodrich
VERSE: David Goodrich

First Sunday after Pentecost/Trinity Sunday A

140